Let's Heal the World

Let's Heal the World

A joint effort in eradicating pornography

Victoria Jonah

authorHOUSE®

AuthorHouse™ UK Ltd.
1663 Liberty Drive
Bloomington, IN 47403   USA
www.authorhouse.co.uk
Phone: 0800.197.4150

Published by AuthorHouse   07/16/2013

ISBN: 978-1-4817-7579-3 (sc)
ISBN: 978-1-4817-7580-9 (e)

DEDICATION

To Vicky, my best friend,
For your constant support in all I do
For giving me a shoulder to lean on
For always believing in me
Thank you.

CONTENTS

Chapter One

THE STALE AIR

The air we breathe smells, and this odour is so stale that after a while, we got ourselves accustomed to it; we are now so use to it that we can't tell the difference. But of course, it does not mean that it is not harming our health.

The adaptation of this decay is going to be for just a while before we start getting very ill. These illnesses are societal menace from this staleness, which is pornography.

Pornography is taking over the society gradually and it seems to be everywhere you look; on media of various kinds like in the movies, soft sell magazine, on the internet, in books, on song lyrics and even on the streets. It permeates gradually into the society and now the society is so helpless about it.

The several ills that pornography brings to our adorable society includes rape, abuse of different kinds, broken homes due to sexual escapades, unnecessary high libido, etc. All these and lots more result to Sex! Sex!! Sex!!!, and of course unprotected and carefree sex because of the surge in the hormone; at the long run, it results to several sexually transmitted diseases (STD's), which one of them is the global health problem, which is Human Immunodeficiency Virus (HIV) and Acquired Immune Deficiency Syndrome (AIDS), which of course is majorly caused by sexual activities of various kinds.

No wonder the **Bible says:**

> **Know ye not that your bodies are the members of Christ? Shall I then take the members of Christ, and make *them* the members of a harlot? God forbid.**

> **What? Know ye not that he which is joined to a harlot is one body? For two saith he shall be one flesh.**

> **But he that is joined unto the Lord is one spirit.**

> **Flee fornication. Every sin that a man doeth is without the body; but he that committed fornication sinneth against his own body.**

> **What? know ye not that you body is the temple of the Holy Ghost *which is* in you, which ye have of God, and ye are not your own?**

> **For ye are bought with a price: therefore glorify God in your body, and in your spirit, which are God's.**

> **I Corinthians 6 vs 15-20 (KJV)**

Let's hear what **D. H Lawrence, a British writer (1885-1930) said about pornography "Porn is the attempt to insult sex, to do dirt on it".** And **Susan Sontag,** a U.S writer quoted that **"what porn is really about, ultimately isn't sex but death"**

We should learn from the Bible, and of course the view of these two and many more that shed light on the dangers of pornography, and let's work together in cleaning our society of the disaster that pornography has already caused us individually and collectively.

I am not about to heap blame on anybody, but suggest ways in which we can get rid of this nuisance together. After all, we have all contributed to making the air stale because of the intense of pornography.

We have one way or the other consciously or unconsciously, directly or indirectly, actively or passively participated in the act of pornography by encouraging it openly or secretly.

Chapter Two

THE BLEAK FUTURE

Before we go on discussing ways that pornography can be eradicated from our society, let us see what the future of our wards or children hold with the speed at which porn is growing in the society.

Can you bear to see your little girl or boy being raped? Can you bear to see your loved ones being abused severely, or suffer from HIV/AIDS, and other STD's, knowing that there are sure maintenance for these illnesses, but what about the pain that they pass through, or the stigma that the society subject them to? What about the death some of them finally results into.

You wonder what this has gotten to do with pornography. It has all to do with it, because a sexually aggressive fellow looses all kinds of reasoning, the only language they understand at that point is **SEX!** either willingly or not.

With the strength of pornography now in our society, its growth might not be measurable though, because it is not every one that gets involve in porn that will open up. But the sure thing is that, if not controlled and finally eradicated from our society, it will gradually get out of hand.

This might result in lots and lots of rapes and abuses, uncontrolled rate of HIV/AIDS, other sexual harassments and several other assaults and torture on these innocent ones.

We have to start planning for the future of our children and wards now. This is as important as investing our time and money in their education, future career and general upbringing.

Fighting against pornography individually is great; after all, little drops of water makes mighty ocean. However, joining hands with other individuals and organizations that work towards eradicating pornography will yield an explosive result in making the society a better one.

As you flip on pages, you'll get more suggestions on what is expected of you and of course, this is not a theory, but a revelation to ways in which you can fight these menace.

> **"The product of the future depends on the preparation of today"—Victoria Jonah**

> **"The future that we study and plan for begins today"—Fischer**

No wonder the **Bible says:**

> **Abstain from all appearance of evil.**
> **1 Thessalonians 5:22 (KJV)**

Having this in mind, what plans are you making in seeing that your lovely children, wards and even younger relations get the best of life? What are you going to do in seeing that the future generation gets the secured and moral society they are entitled to? However you want to go about it, always put this verse in mind, don't get them involved in anything that "appears like evil" saying it doesn't matter, because it does a great deal.

Now do you feel like stopping, because this kind of book is "not your thing" It is two sides of the coin; either you read on and find out what is expected of you, in preserving this society or you stop reading and shrug off, saying "it's none of my business" either ways, the preservation and cleansing of the society lies in your hands.

Chapter Three
SHOW BIZ

Entertainment is a very tactful job, done by talented people, who dedicate their time, energy and pleasure to give people relaxation and amusement. Believe me, composing songs and playwriting is no joke, so is acting, dancing and singing.

There is no doubt that there are several wonderful people in this so famous industry all over the world. It has of course been in existence for long and beautiful people have graced this industry.

The entertainment industry educates the general populace one-way or the other; after all, entertainment is educative.

Show biz as an act of entertainment has several segments. However, the two major ones, which are music and movie, are the ones I will be discussing in this chapter.

Movie and musical video does not have to show sexual scenes before they entertain, do they? They don't have to reveal the animalistic behavior of humans before they become appealing to viewers.

Let's hear the view of these two philosophers on music. According to **Carlyle, "Music is well said to be the speech of angels".** Does that mean that angels writes or speaks dirty languages or write dirty lyrics like the ones that we often hear in most of our music today? According to **Longfellow, "Music is the Universal language of mankind".** Does that mean that the only language that man speaks includes lyrics that corrupt minds? Music is supposed to be educative and entertaining.

> **But there is a spirit in man: and the inspiration of the Almighty giveth them understanding.**
>
> **Great men are not always wise: neither do the aged understand judgment. Job 32: 8-9 (KJV)**

There is no "know it all" you cannot be the Mr. Prefect in the industry.

Like I earlier said that show biz is very demanding, and the motive is to entertain and educate.

What kind of education or entertainment do you have in mind, because, the education might be negative or positive.

There is need to talk about entertainment and education because this is very important to human development. No wonder **Marshall McLuhan (1911-1980)** quoted that **"it is misleading to suppose there's any basic difference between education and entertainment"**

Let's talk to our conscience; as a script or song writer, what does your script tells the audience? Is it encouraging porn in the society while it entertains or discourages it? Is it grooming the younger generation on how to be "cool" even if it has to do with abusing, harassing or assaulting their mates or even older ones sexually.

As an actor, actress or musician, what kind of script do you act, what kind of costume do you wear. Do you really have to show the world how endowed you are? Do you have to abuse the mind of sane and decent people, by making them fantasize about having sex with you and how sexually active you could be?

Don't you think that it is not necessary exposing your body, while singing or acting almost nude on the stage, getting involved in sex scenes and the likes, because **YOU ARE BEAUTIFUL**; even without revealing pounds of flesh, talk less of posing nude? Aren't you supposed to preserve that beauty and glow, instead of trying so hard to be noticed by being so uncivilized with animalistic behavior?

Are you asking what should I do? Be modest and decent in all you do and the positive result will amaze everyone, even you. Isn't that why God gave us a "blank cheque" in the Bible? To ask for wisdom when we come short of it?

> **If any of you lack wisdom, let him ask of God, that giveth to all men liberally, and upbraideth not; and it shall be given him.**
> **James 1:5 (KJV)**

The fact that you are a public figure and sophisticated makes people look up to you, and the rate at which you inspire and influences them cannot be over emphasized.

However, change is a personal thing; make up your mind to be the change that the world needs.

Chapter Four
WORLD WIDE WEB AND PORN

Technology is reshaping this economy and transforming businesses and consumers. This is about more than e-commerce, or e-mail, or e-trades, or e-files. It is about the 'e' in economic opportunity.

—William Daley (1951-)

World Wide Web is one of the outcomes of technology and the benefit cannot be overemphasized. There are too many good that internet has introduced to mankind. Part of it is the e-transact, that enables you get involved in several type of transaction online. e-banking, e-mail, shopping online endlessly, social network, that makes people to get involved in several kinds business connection and friendship. Some even got the love of their lives on these social websites, and they are living happily.

With all these examples and lots more that you already know of, we are double certain that internet facilities is a very great success in the world technology.

Is there anything that has a good side without the bad side? Even if it has bad side, must we get involved in the bad aspects of it? These questions can be answered by you alone.

Richard Norgaard (1943-) has these to say about technology **"As we push our technologies to exploit more and more resources, we now recognize that unforeseen consequences are becoming increasingly global in nature"**

Permit me to say that some of us are abusing the World Wide Web by using it for things that are not decent, like sending nude pictures on the web, which is far from being cool and dignified. We not only pollute ourselves, but we pollute others as well. We reduce ourselves to object of ridicule and mockery because people that does this has low self esteem and they are fighting so hard to get attention; did they get it? I don't think so, because the attention is negative, it does not worth it, it is not what ordinarily they can be proud of, neither is it what the society or their relation can give them a thumb up for. Nobody in its right senses will say a bravo to someone with these shameful and scandalous acts.

It takes a person that is not in their right senses to get involve in internet sex escapades. It is absurd for someone to undress, and reveal their greatest treasure which is their body to everyone to explore. That means they are nothing but a mere specimen for all to see.

You want to ask me about those that actually get involved in the act of sleeping with each other and showing the whole world how they can be animalistic? Anyway, that is twice as bad as the act of posing nude and showing off your private parts.

Is it too late to make amendment? NEVER; it is not too late. No matter how deeply involved you are in these act; the beauty of it is that there is nobody that cannot change and be the change that the world needs.

> **Bible says: For I have no pleasure in the death of him that dieth, saith the Lord GOD: wherefore turn yourselves, and live ye. Ezekiel 18:32 (KJV)**

After all, this book is about "healing the world" the singular act of you changing, goes a long way in **HEALING THE WORLD.**

Chapter Five

HIGHBROW AND PORN

It is not easy to be a high brow. It takes a very creative, serious, cultured, intellectual mind to be one. The highbrow I am referring to here are the brilliant writers, intelligent photographers, super cartoonist, outstanding advertisers . . .

I cannot exhaust the list of these wonderful people, who keep the world going with what they do. They keep the world enlightened, educated, colourful and beautiful; and this, I must confess it is a great task.

In every profession, there are people that always go to the extreme, doing what is not the ethics of the profession. The motive behind what each highbrow does goes a long way to tell much about the personality of the person.

The author of soft sell magazine, showing pictures of nude people to stimulate the general public has a lot to tell about his or her personality.

What is the intention of the advertiser that uses provocative pictures to negatively stimulate the general public? There is much to what each and every one of us does; it affects people positively or negatively.

People are stimulated, and their sexual drive increases so speedily. Some even want to practice crazy sex because of all the sexual exposure they get from the highbrow, and they go to the extent of getting pharmaceutical sexual stimulant to boost their libido, because of the psychological harm that some of this supposed highbrow have done to them.

No wonder **Elizabeth 1 (1533-1603)** has this to say about the highbrow that are doing it the other way round. **"I muse how men of wit can so hardly use that gift they hold"**

Wouldn't you rather use your gift wisely, as a cartoonist, wouldn't you rather use your gift to entertain and thrill the cartoon lovers, rather that wearing them down and driving them crazy sexually.

I really love watching cartoon and I have watch one that shocked me, when I saw sexual scene in the cartoon, I mean two of the characters making out, and I was frightened. Since cartoon is majorly know as the choice of the younger generation, then who is spared, if the cartoonist cannot spare the children "the major cartoon lovers" then who is safe from this menace.

As a photographer, graphic designer and the likes, what is it that thrills you? What is it that makes you want to do more and more? Your attitude will definitely be reflected in your design and pictures taken.

As a model, what kind of jobs do you do? Wouldn't you rather be known for decent work, than works that can corrupt the future of tomorrow and the society as a whole?

> **You can detect them by the way they act, just as you can identify a tree by its fruit. You don't pick grapes from thornbushes, or figs from thistles.**
>
> **A healthy tree produces good fruit, and an unhealthy tree produces bad fruit.**
>
> **A good tree can't produce bad fruit, and a bad tree can't produce good fruit.**
>
> **So every tree that does not produce good fruit is chopped down and thrown into the fire.**
>
> **Yes, the way to identify a tree or a person is by the kind of fruit that is produced.**
>
> **Matthew 7:16-20 (NLT)**

With all these that I have talked about, can you still classify yourself as been a highbrow? Oh yes! You are still a highbrow, so you are really educating the people and beautifying the world positively.

What about someone you know? Friend, colleague, neighbour or an acquaintant that does the polluting with his or her creativity. Why not talk to such a fellow, educate the fellow so that the world will really be healed from all the ills that porn is causing.

I know this cannot happen in just a day, it is gradual. It can start with you stopping the world from going to total decay, either by stopping a friend that is deeply buried in such act or your very self stopping it. But if you still insist on polluting the world with your creativity, you are proving to be an intellectual betrayal.

Chapter Six

MY BODY AND I

"And there isn't any way that one can get rid of the guilt of having a nice body by saying that one can serve society with it, because that would end up, with one self as what? There simply doesn't seem to be any moral place for flesh"

—Margaret Drabble (1939-)

Stripping is another form of pornography and it is actually used as occupation by some people, who thought is the only way they can make ends meet.

I am not here to condemn anybody for turning into a stripper, because if you ask one million people that strips, they will give you ten million different reasons why they ended up stripping. Some of these reasons are very pathetic; infact, some will actually bring tears to your eyes.

I want to believe that there are still ways in which people can earn their living, in a decent way. Though the money they get might not be as much as the ones they will get when they strip, but the stripping money has all sorts of moral filth and humiliation on it. And most especially, it takes away ones self-worth.

Even though the strippers might not admit this openly, but I want to believe that if they are given a better opportunity, majority will prefer it to stripping. They will prefer a job that they can boldly tell people about.

Earning a living is important and so is adding skills and values to our life from time to time, so that at each point, we can be relevant in the society and our services or goods will be needed.

There are several vocations that one can learn within a short period and earn a decent living, rather than earning a living by stripping or having sex on a stage, or in the public for viewers to get erotic.

Why must it be you and your body that will be used as a tool to quench the sexual thirst of those people that thinks they can always pay for your sexual display?

Your body should be treated with respect and not as a trade tool. It is more dignifying to earn a dollar decently than to earn hundreds of dollars humiliating your body.

If you think you can continue to serve the general public with your body, then you are contradicting the Bible and the general believe.

> **What? know ye not that your body is the temple of the Holy Ghost which is in you,**

> **which ye have of God, and ye are not your**
> **own? 1 Corinthians 6:19 (KJV)**

Your body is really sacred and should be treated as one, and not as a public property, where anybody can have asses to.

> **"If anything is sacred the human body is**
> **sacred"**
>
> **—Walt Whitman (1819-1892)**

Listen, not only your private part is a private property, but the whole of your body.

Chapter Seven
THE MIRROR

Children have never been very good at listening to their elders but they have never fail to imitate them.

—James Baldwin

It is just so natural for our children to imitate us, because we are the mirror they have grown to know. They imitate our day to day life styles so well that one will begin to wonder if they are not our cloned self.

To our children, it doesn't matter if our attitude is positive or negative, right or wrong; they just go on imitating them. These attitudes of ours that our children are imitating, can either make or mar their future.

Some parents do not lay good examples; they still leave the reckless and carefree life they were used to when they were not yet a parent, habits that are not healthy for the growth and development of children, simply because they are not yet ready to become a parent.

They are not just ready for the responsibilities of parenthood, before they are saddled with it.

Some even became a parent due to one of the menace caused by pornography, which is rape. Such a victim that got pregnant and had a baby through rape cannot be qualified as a ready parent. A high school young man that got his girlfriend pregnant and they ended up with a child is not yet ready, so is the girl that was impregnated.

That brings in mind the quotation of a British Psychologist and writer, **Penelope Leach which says "Kids haven't changed much, but parents seems increasingly unhappy with the child raising phase of their lives".**

What does this bring to your mind, especially if you have found yourself in this shoe? Was it not the carefree sex you had, because your libido could not listen to your reasoning any longer? Was it not that movie that inspired it, or was yours that lady that dresses so provocatively that you admire secretly that gave you such a jump in sex that made you lose the entire grip that you had before. Oh, is yours that song lyrics that so turned you on, to the extent that you could not resist that wayward friend of yours, until you started having sex together, letting go all your reasoning.

Maybe it is the types of books you read that put the clear picture on your mind and all you want to do is carry it out. You just want to get laid; it does not matter to you, how or with whom it is done, all you just want was to carry it out.

Is one of these your story? Or is it so related. Hmm, this is the story of majority. Getting turned on because of the rate of pornography that is everywhere in our society and they end up making the wrong decision.

Come to think of it, can you stand your child passing through the same thing you passed through? History might repeat itself due to your negative influence on them, and you, not making them to live up to the supposed moral standard.

Yours might even be that you were so spoilt; you had all it takes to make the world go round, so, you seize the opportunity to live life in its fullness, by living recklessly. And then, things went out of hand for you, you became porn suggestive, because of the type of friends you bring home, the kind of crazy party you throw and your vulgarity in general.

Maybe you think this child does not deserve to be treated so specially because he or she is a love child or out of wedlock child. You are getting it all wrong because every child needs to be treated special because they are different and special persons with special destiny and have nothing to do with how the father has denied the pregnancy or how you were treated badly, or even how your own parent treated you when you were about same age.

What does the Bible has to say about EVERY CHILD

Children are a gift from the Lord; they are a reward from Him. Psalm 127:3 (NLT)

It doesn't matter if they are love children, disabled, good looking, dull, brilliant or not. All children are heritage of the Lord and should be treated with loads and loads of love.

If you really love someone, you won't hurt them. If you love your child/children/ward(s), you will lay good examples, having it in mind that you are their mirror.

Does it now mean that it is only the young parents that are not ready for parenting?, not at all, it has permeates into the society at large, just that the teenagers seems to fall into these categories the most.

Parents are to dress decently so that they will be the role model their wards needs, and not dressing in a provocative way. Dressing decently does not actually means dressing oddly.

There are several beautiful outfits that well known designers have for those parents that like wearing classy designers' attires. There are other designers that are not well known as well that has very beautiful attires that are not pornographic, revealing all ones private parts/features.

Parents are to be at alert, censoring the kinds of movie their children watches, minding the type they watch when they are around them, minding the type of music they listen to, the type of story books they buy for them and even the types of cloths they buy for their children and wards. This is because when you buy revealing and seductive cloths for your children, thinking they don't have the type of body that will attract the opposite sex now; when they start growing into a stunning beauty, be it male or female, having that kind of body that is innocent but beautiful, they would have already cultivate the habit of dressing indecently, then it can be difficult changing them.

This is because the habit we form gradually goes a long way in telling the person we finally become.

As parents, whatever age grade we are, or profession we practice, we should note that we are the mirror, guidelines and example that our children follow. If as a parent, we do not set good example, our children are at the risk of falling astray.

If as parents, we live good example, we will prevent several ills from happening to our wards, ills like rape, sexual assault, sexual harassment, which are parts of the consequences of bad clothing

Other ills are depression, wildness, aggressiveness, poor performance at school due to divided attention, teenage pregnancy, which affects the boys and the girls as well.

We can now see that we have nothing to lose by living rightly and be a role model for our children, wards and even the society at large. On the other hand, we have everything to lose by living a careless and reckless life.

Let's continue to see our children as our sole responsibility, not as some aliens that has come to stay for a while and obstruct our lives. Not even as just a friend that can come and go some day. But as a gift from God, as a sunlight that brightens our world, as a beauty to our lives, and the joy that gladdens our souls, and as a permanent tie to us and our destiny.

Chapter Eight

PORN AND HUMAN TRAFFICKING

Could you have seen that mother clinging to her child, when they fastened the iron upon his wrist; could you have heard her heart-rending groans, and seen her bloodshot eyes wander wildly from face to face, vainly pleading for mercy; could you have witness that scene as I saw it, you would exclaim, slavery is damnable!

—Harriet Ann Jacobs

The act of using enforced labour on someone has been assumed to have been eradicated all along. Contrary to the claim, it is still very on and one of the major reason why it is still in vogue is because of the menace of pornography.

Slavery is condemned, because it is an act of wickedness, while some people pardon porn, even when it is sex slavery, which is forced on the participants.

The truth is that, when porn is totally eradicated, human trafficking will naturally reduced. You want to know why? The high patronage of sex trade (girls/young women) which victims are majorly kidnapped for will reduce extremely.

Ordinarily, people with normal libido will not go about looking for just anybody to satisfy their urge. It is when someone feels so explosive because of all the nude pictures, half naked adverts, dirty lyrics, sex scenes movies, bad parental influence and the likes; that the person is ready to just have sex, no matter what it takes, who it hurts and what it cost.

Such people go about patronizing motels, strip clubs, Websites for meeting active sexual partners and the list is endless; just to have the pleasure they feel they have been deprived.

These set of people go to any length to satisfy their urge, not minding who or what they have it with, or even how they have it.

No wonder **Saul Bellow, a U.S writer said this about sex "Erotic practices have been diversified, Sex used to be a single-crop farming, like cotton or wheat, now people raise all sort of things"**

The traffickers in turn have forgotten this truth:

> **Be not deceived; God is not mocked: for whatsoever a man soweth, that shall he also reap. Galatians 6:7 (KJV)**

What the traffickers are yet to learn is that, what goes around comes around. They can never go scot free from all their ills act; nemesis will definitely catch up with them.

Human Traffickers have lots of drugged sexual workers which they make available for these categories of mostly men that want pleasure at whatever stake.

It has gone beyond the fact that the trafficker patronizes just one or two continents only, now they are all over, in every continents, girls and young women disappears every now and then and are trafficked for sex trade. At times, it might even be within one continent, it doesn't have to be so far apart.

Others that cannot afford to pay for sex can get crazy and ambush girls, kidnap them and then rape them and have them for keep as long as they want to satisfy their urges until they are tired of such person and then dispose. If the victim is lucky, but if unlucky, they murder her, and the circle goes on and on.

People that act with such level of tyranny does not put in mind that

> **"It is better that a man should tyrannize over his bank balance than over his fellow citizens"**
>
> **—John Maynard Keynes (1883-1946)**

Come to think of it, people's sexual urge cannot become so irrational if they are not spurred just unnecessarily by several forms of pornography.

We can now see that fighting porn that has eaten deep into our society is a two way weapon here as we will be fighting against human trafficking as well eradicating pornographic as a whole.

Chapter Nine

OUR SOCIETY AND PORN

N0 drugs, not even alcohol, causes the fundamental ills of the society. If we're looking for sources of our troubles, we shouldn't test people for drugs, we should test them for stupidity, ignorance, greed, and love of power

—P. J. O'Rourke (1947-)

Society at large is a part of one's life that can never be ignored, no matter how hard one tries to isolate one's self, one is still part of the society.

Staying in a terrain that involves several thousand kilometers without a neighbor is not even enough to cut anyone off the society.

I am just saying this to lay emphasis on the importance of the society. Don't get me wrong, I know you already know society is important, but how important is the society to you?

This is a one zillion dollar question; the society which is the social relationships among different or group of people is unavoidable. It is very important to note that the society is very important to you, just as it had been to your previous generations and how it will still be to your coming generations.

There are some people who before now holds a very huge value to their societal values and that is very good. Such people can choose their residential area, the kind of people they relate with, the kind of school their wards attends, the kinds of party they attend, even the place they do their shopping . . . the list is inexhaustible, and if I am not mistaking, that person is YOU.

One thing that you do not take serious is the kind of growth or changes your society is undergoing. Did I hear you laugh, saying you cannot do anything about it, blaming the government, or the nongovernmental organizations, or blaming the influential people.

Let's go to this mind trip together, when we get back, you will tell if you can do something about your societal values or not.

Imagine your immediate society, where things are not too out of hand, where you can at least experience some peace of mind, oh, if you don't experience peace in your neighbourhood, then, am sure you are there because you don't have any option, not that you really like it; so let's just take it now that your society is peaceful.

Imagine waking up in the morning and discovering that in your so peaceful lifestyle, you peeped from the window and discovered several mates having sex, and as you try to clean your eyes, to wake up from this horrible dream, you turned to look ahead into the street, and everywhere you look, you see people nude, having nothing but sex, in short, this involves the underage, I mean children. You want to brace yourself that it is okay with your own standard and you went in to say hi to you supposed innocent children and lo and behold, they are nude, smooching each other . . . did I hear you scream . . . especially when they are not remorseful about it. If you think that is okay too, and you went to have your bath to go to the office, just on your pouch, you saw a neighbor making out with your supposed pet animal . . . you think this is mere exaggeration?, no, is it not, if porn keeps growing speedily, it will gradually get to this.

Imagine the growth of porn in the next 10 years, what people will wear, the value they will place on illicit sex . . . are you with me? Now think of the next 20 years, the level of craziness about sex, the level of rape . . . are you still there? Now imagine the next 50 years, 100 years, when our children are grand and great grand, the level of sexual harassment, abuse, violence and assault. Imagine how radiant, beautiful and colourful that porn will be appearing in the previous years if not controlled . . . of course, it is going to be coat of many colours with golden tiara, with the most beautiful studs of diamonds all over, and think of how our society will be . . . it will rots with the worst of stenches combine together, it will be so unsecured to the extent that you will be so scared to leave your kids of same sex together, talk less of the opposite sex, nor will you want them to go school, because everywhere you go, people will be making out. This will not leave out children of any age.

Even children of as young as innocence will be getting laid and the society will be so decayed.

This does not leave out diseases like HIV/AIDS and probably some more deadier sexually transmitted diseases will be discovered then.

I know every normal person cannot stand this state of decay in the society and what option are we left with? HEALING THE WORLD of porn is the duty of all of us, it is my job, your job and our job to fight this menace and prevent it from destroying our society, if not, the next generation will curse us for allowing this menace to choke them and turn them into sex slaves.

> **Then if my people who are called by my name will humble themselves and pray and seek my face and turn from their wicked ways, I will hear from heaven and will forgive their sins and heal their land. 2Chronicles 7:14 (NLT)**

Chapter Ten

THE RECOVERY

Reform never comes to a class or a people
unless and until those concern have worked
out their own salvation

—Joseph Ephraim Casely-Hayford
(1866-1930)

Imagine a world free of porn . . .

You think it is not possible? Okay, let your
imagination do the job, after all **"imagination . . . is
the irrepressible revolutionist"—Wallace Stevens
(1879-1955)**

Let's imagine a world free of porn, where everyone
dresses in a decent manner, where there are no dirty
song lyrics, no dirty movies, no ill adverts, and the list
of porn of course is endless.

Now, let's imagine a world free of porn. Did I hear you
say that will be in heaven? No! Not at all; it doesn't have
to be that way. When the world is free from porn, then
it will be free from several sexually transmitted diseases
(STD's), free from rape, all sourts of sexual harassment,
sexual assaults and all the likes.

The world will be a place where people will always seek for decency. I am not saying everybody will buy this idea, I am not saying everybody want to be decent, after all, it is only sane people that can be decent. When the majority believes in changing the world, not just for themselves, but as well as for the upcoming generation, then the world will be a better place.

The power of our imagination cannot be underestimated, dream change the world and change come when people dream. Dream a world free from pornography of every kind, a world where the future generation can appreciate and not depreciate.

In dreaming, action will take place eventually, because the zeal to make the changes take place will spur the changes, and we will find ourselves wanting that picture that our mind has created and then we will start practicing it.

> **I am enough of an artist to draw freely upon my imagination. Imagination is more important than knowledge. Knowledge is limited. Imagination encircles the world.**
> **—Albert Einstein (1879-1955)**

The world is meant to be a beautiful place, let's work together and make it beautiful inside out, let's puts our hands together and **HEAL THE WORLD**.

> **Do not let sin control the way you live; do not give in to its lustful desires.**

Do not let any part of your body become a tool of wickedness, to be used for sinning. Instead, give yourselves completely to God since you have been given new life. And use your whole body as a tool to do what is right for the glory of God.

Sin is no longer your master, for you are no longer subject to the law, which enslaves you to sin. Instead, you are free by God's grace.

So since God's grace has set us free from the law, does this mean we can go on sinning? Of course not!

Don't you realize that whatever you choose to obey becomes your master? You can choose sin, which leads to death, or you can choose to obey God and receive his approval.

Romans 6:12-16 (NLT)

THE CHANGES I DESIRE

Imagine and write down the changes you desire in the following aspects and work towards achieving them

- **Your day to day activities**

  _____
  _____
  _____
  _____
  _____

- **Your choice of movie and music**

  _____
  _____
  _____
  _____
  _____

- **Your choice of cloths**

  _____
  _____
  _____
  _____
  _____

- **Your choice of relaxation activities**

  _____
  _____
  _____
  _____
  _____

- **Your choice of music and movies.**

  _____
  _____
  _____
  _____
  _____

- **Add others**

  _____
  _____
  _____
  _____
  _____
  _____
  _____
  _____
  _____
  _____
  _____
  _____
  _____
  _____
  _____
  _____

_____

_____

Have a positive attitude towards change and it will come.

ABOUT THE AUTHOR

Victoria Jonah is a refined author who has published a couple of books locally and coauthored academic books with polished academician via renowned publisher.

Other educational, moral, and spiritual books meant to reform the society at large are part of her accomplishments.

The author of Teenagers Prayer Book, published by Authorhouse, is a master's degree holder in educational management from the University of Ibadan. She is also a teenagers' church coordinator and a Sunday schoolteacher.

She presently resides in Nigeria with her family.